초등 영어독해를 쉽고 재미있게!

똑똑한 초등영어독해 Starter 2 [개정판]

초등 영어독해를 쉽고 재미있게!
똑똑한 초등영어독해 Starter 2 [개정판]

2007년 12월 18일 초판 1쇄 발행
2023년 12월 18일 개정 1쇄 인쇄
2023년 12월 25일 개정 1쇄 발행

지은이 국제어학연구소 영어학부
감수 Jenny Kim
그림 유지환
펴낸이 이규인
펴낸곳 국제어학연구소 출판부

출판등록 2010년 1월 18일 제302-2010-000006호
주소 서울특별시 마포구 대흥로4길 49, 1층(용강동 월명빌딩)
Tel (02) 704-0900 **팩시밀리** (02) 703-5117
홈페이지 www.bookcamp.co.kr
e-mail changbook1@hanmail.net

ISBN 979-11-9792037-0 13740
정가 13,000원

영어의 기초를 다져 주는
magic 시리즈

초등 영어 독해를 쉽고 재미있게!

똑똑한

Starter 2

초등 **영어독해**

개정판

글 국제어학연구소 영어학부 | **감수** Jenny Kim | **그림** 유지환

ILR 국제어학연구소

머리말

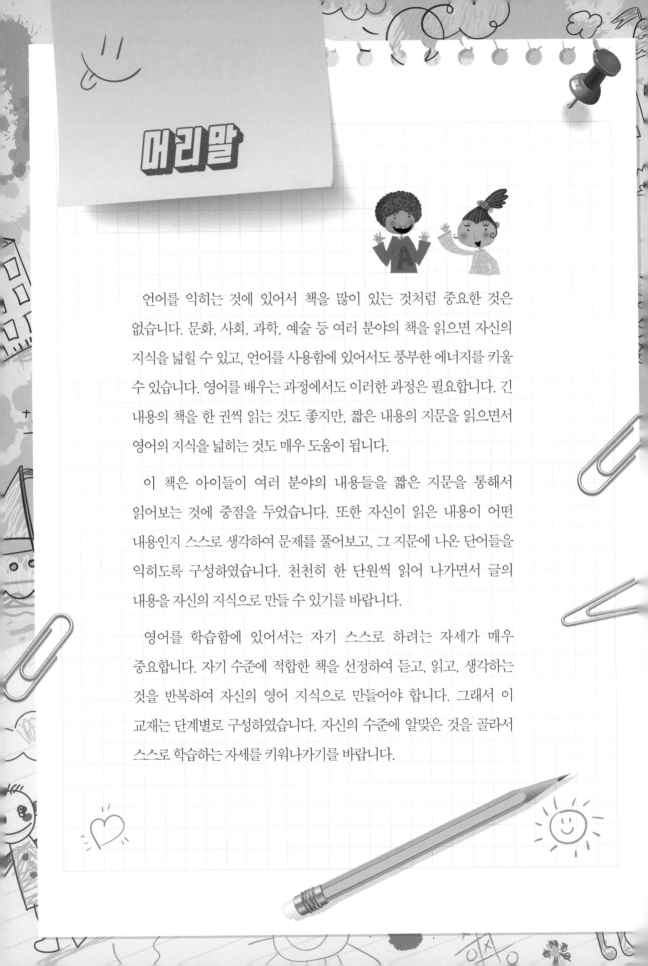

언어를 익히는 것에 있어서 책을 많이 있는 것처럼 중요한 것은 없습니다. 문화, 사회, 과학, 예술 등 여러 분야의 책을 읽으면 자신의 지식을 넓힐 수 있고, 언어를 사용함에 있어서도 풍부한 에너지를 키울 수 있습니다. 영어를 배우는 과정에서도 이러한 과정은 필요합니다. 긴 내용의 책을 한 권씩 읽는 것도 좋지만, 짧은 내용의 지문을 읽으면서 영어의 지식을 넓히는 것도 매우 도움이 됩니다.

이 책은 아이들이 여러 분야의 내용들을 짧은 지문을 통해서 읽어보는 것에 중점을 두었습니다. 또한 자신이 읽은 내용이 어떤 내용인지 스스로 생각하여 문제를 풀어보고, 그 지문에 나온 단어들을 익히도록 구성하였습니다. 천천히 한 단원씩 읽어 나가면서 글의 내용을 자신의 지식으로 만들 수 있기를 바랍니다.

영어를 학습함에 있어서는 자기 스스로 하려는 자세가 매우 중요합니다. 자기 수준에 적합한 책을 선정하여 듣고, 읽고, 생각하는 것을 반복하여 자신의 영어 지식으로 만들어야 합니다. 그래서 이 교재는 단계별로 구성하였습니다. 자신의 수준에 알맞은 것을 골라서 스스로 학습하는 자세를 키워나가기를 바랍니다.

이 책의 구성

Before Reading

스토리에 대한 이해도를 높이기 위하여 새로운 단어와 중요 표현을 미리 익혀요.

Story

앞에서 배운 단어와 표현을 생각하면서 스토리를 이해해요.

Vocabulary

선잇기를 통해 배운 단어들을 확인해요.

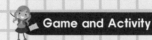

After Reading

스토리를 얼마나 이해했는지 자신의 실력을 체크해 봐요.

Game and Activity

재미있는 게임문제를 풀면서 단어를 복습해요.

차례

Unit 1 What time is it? 9

Unit 2 Where do animals live? 15

Unit 3 Are you tired? 21

Unit 4 I can sing a song. 27

Unit 5 Are you a monster? 33

Unit 6 Christmas gift 39

Unit 7 Knock, knock 45

Unit 8 Rabbits 51

Unit 9 Look at me! 57

Unit 10 4 seasons 63

Unit 11   A salad ————————————————— 69

Unit 12   Put on your mittens. ———————————— 75

Unit 13   In the sea ———————————————— 81

Unit 14   I have many pets. ————————————— 87

Unit 15   Yummy! ———————————————— 93

Unit 16   It is mine. ———————————————— 99

Unit 17   The birthday party ————————————— 105

Unit 18   It is sweet. ———————————————— 111

Unit 19   They are so cute! ————————————— 117

Unit 20   What shape is this? ———————————— 123

스토리 해석 및 정답 —————————————————— 129

Before Reading

New Words 새 단어

time

seven

hurry

dad

ten

sleepy

Key Expression 주요 표현

A: What time is it?
B: It's ten o'clock.

A: What _____ is it?

B: It's two o'clock.

Story

What time is it?

What time is it, Mom?
It's seven o'clock.
Time to go to school!
Oh, I have to hurry.
What time is it, Dad?
It's ten o'clock.
Time to go to bed!
I'm so sleepy.

Vocabulary

Match the Words 낱말 연결하기

1  •   • hurry

2  •   • ten

3  •   • seven

4  •   • sleepy

5  •   • time

6  •   • dad

After Reading

Look and Choose 그림 보고 고르기

①

A: What time is it?

B: It's seven _____ .

    a. o'clock   b. time   c. clock

②

_____ to go to bed.

a. It   b. Time   c. I'm

③

I'm _____ sleepy.

a. to   b. my   c. so

Think and Choose 문장 읽고 고르기

① What time does the girl go to school?

    a. six   b. seven   c. eight

② What time does the girl go to bed?

    a. nine   b. ten   c. eleven

Look and Write 그림 보고 쓰기

| ten | hurry | seven | dad | time | sleepy |

What ❶ _____ is it, Mom?

It's ❷ _____ o'clock.

Time to go to school!
Oh, I have to ❸ _____ .

What time is it, ❹ _____ ?

It's ❺ _____ o'clock.

Time to go to bed!
I'm so ❻ _____ .

Game and Activity

 그림으로 제시된 단어들을 찾아서 표시하세요.

① 　　② 　　③

s	l	x	z	t	a	c
t	e	n	d	i	w	s
q	t	v	k	m	j	❶ h
y	b	h	e	e	i	u
f	z	t	b	n	r	r
r	d	a	d	v	l	r
a	s	l	e	e	p	y

④ 　　⑤ 　　⑥ 10

Before Reading

New Words 새 단어

bat

cave

bee

hive

nest

frog

pond

Key Expression 주요 표현

They live in caves.

❶ They _____ in hives.

❷ They _____ in nests.

❸ They _____ in ponds.

Where do animals live?

Where do bats live?

They live in caves.

Where do bees live?

They live in hives.

Where do birds live?

They live in nests.

Where do frogs live?

They live in ponds.

Match the Words 낱말 연결하기

①  •　　　　　　• frog

②  •　　　　　　• hive

③  •　　　　　　• cave

④  •　　　　　　• pond

⑤  •　　　　　　• bee

⑥  •　　　　　　• nest

After Reading

Look and Choose 그림 보고 고르기

❶

A: _____ do bees live?

B: They live in hives.

    a. Who   b. Where c. What

❷

A: Where do frogs live?

B: _____ live in ponds.

    a. You   b. We   c. They

Think and Choose 문장 읽고 고르기

❶ Where do birds live?

    a. hives   b. ponds   c. nests

❷ Who lives in caves?

    a. bees   b. bats   c. frogs

Look and Write 그림 보고 쓰기

bees   ponds   nests   caves   frogs   hives

Where do bats live?
They live in ❶ _____ .

Where do ❷ _____ live?

They live in ❸ _____ .
Where do birds live?

They live in ❹ _____ .

Where do ❺ _____ live?

They live in ❻ _____ .

Game and Activity

순서가 뒤섞인 알파벳을 알맞게 배열하여 쓰세요.

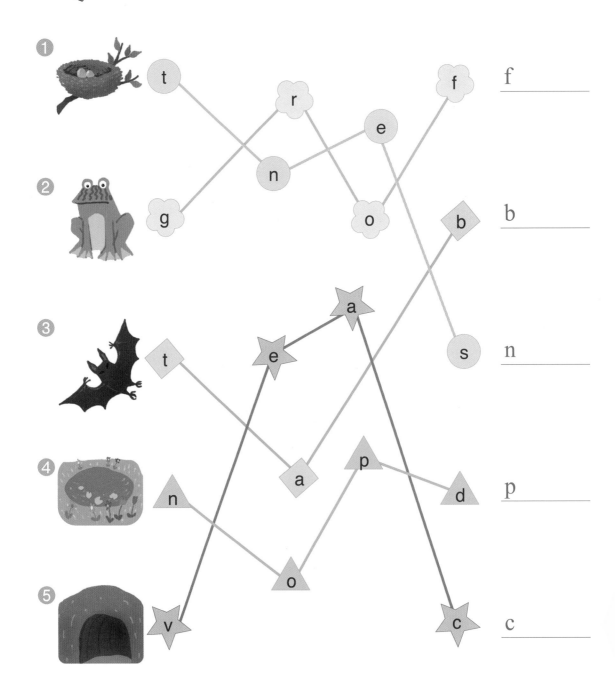

① f _____

② b _____

③ n _____

④ p _____

⑤ c _____

Before Reading

New Words 새 단어

tired

hungry

full

thirsty

sick

angry

Key Expression 주요 표현

A: Are you tired?
B: No, I'm not.

A: _____ you sick?

B: No, I'm not.

 Story

Are you tired?

Are you tired?

No, I'm not.

Are you hungry?

No, I'm not. I'm full.

Are you thirsty?

No, I'm not. I'm sick.

Are you angry?

Yes, I am.

Match the Words 낱말 연결하기

1  •   • hungry

2  •   • tired

3  •   • thirsty

4  •   • angry

5  •   • full

6  •   • sick

After Reading

Write T or F 맞으면T, 틀리면 F

①  I'm full. _____

②   I'm sick. _____

③  I'm hungry. _____

Look and Choose 그림 보고 고르기

①   A: Are you _____?

B: Yes, I am.

    a. full   b. tired   c. angry

②  A: Are you thirsty?

B: No, I'm not. I'm _____.

    a. sick   b. sleepy c. hungry

Look and Write 그림 보고 쓰기

hungry   thirsty   full   tired   sick   angry

Are you ❶ _____ ?
No, I'm not.

Are you ❷ _____ ?

No, I'm not. I'm ❸ _____ .

Are you ❹ _____ ?

No, I'm not. I'm ❺ _____ ?

Are you ❻ _____ .
Yes, I am.

Game and Activity

 그림을 보고 퍼즐의 빈칸을 채우세요.

①

②

③

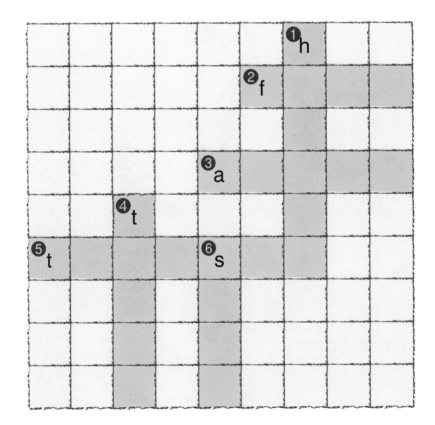

④

⑤

⑥

Before Reading

New Words 새 단어

sing

song

clap

ring

bell

stomp

Key Expression 주요 표현

I can sing a song.

❶ I _____ ring a bell.

❷ I _____ clap.

❸ I _____ stomp.

I can sing a song.

I can sing a song.

La, la! La, la!

Sally can clap.

Clap, clap! Clap, clap!

Sam can ring a bell.

Ding dong! Ding dong!

We can stomp.

Stomp stomp! Stomp stomp!

Match the Words 낱말 연결하기

①  •

• bell

②  •

• sing

③  •

• clap

④  •

• ring

⑤  •

• song

⑥  •

• stomp

After Reading

Look and Choose 그림 보고 고르기

1

We can _____.

a. clap   b. stomp   c. ring

2

He can _____ a bell.

a. ring   b. sing   c. call

3

I can sing a _____.

a. song   b. picture   c. music

Think and Choose 문장 읽고 고르기

1 Who can sing a song?

a. they   b. she   c. I

2 Who can ring a bell?

a. Sally   b. Sam   c. I

Look and Write 그림 보고 쓰기

| clap | stomp | sing | bell | song | ring |

I can ❶_____ a ❷_____.

La, la! La, la!

Sally can ❸_____.

Clap, clap! Clap, clap!

Sam can ❹_____ a ❺_____.

Ding dong! Ding dong!

We can ❻_____.

Stomp stomp! Stomp stomp!

Game and Activity

✏️ 사다리를 타고 내려가서 그림에 맞는 단어를 쓰세요.

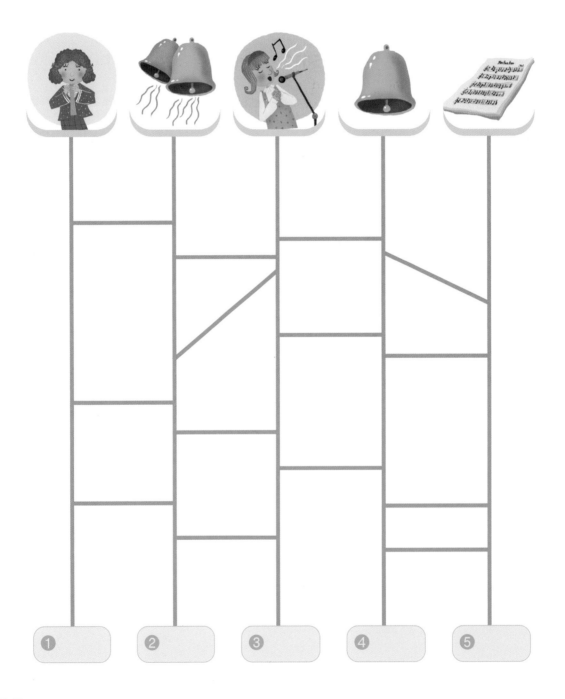

Before Reading

New Words 새 단어

monster

snake

lamb

big

ghost

real

Key Expression 주요 표현

A: Are you a monster?
B: No, I am a snake.

A: Are you a _____?

B: No, I am a lamb.

Are you a monster?

Are you a monster?

No, I'm a snake.

Are you a monster?

No, I'm a lamb.

Are you a monster?

No, I'm a big ghost.

Are you a monster?

Yes, I'm a real monster.

Vocabulary

Match the Words 낱말 연결하기

     •   • monster

    •   • snake

     •   • lamb

     •   • real

     •   • big

   •   • ghost

After Reading

Look and Choose 그림 보고 고르기

1

I'm a _____.

a. tiger   b. ghost   c. lamb

2

A: Are you a monster?

B: No, I'm a _____ ghost.

a. small   b. fat   c. big

3

I'm a _____.

a. snake   b. giraffe   c. lion

Think and Choose 문장 읽고 고르기

1 This story is about _____.

a. me   b. a monkey   c. a monster

2 Is there a real monster?

a. yes   b. no

Look and Write 그림 보고 쓰기

| monster | lamb | big | ghost | snake | real |

Are you a monster?

No, I'm a ❶ _____  .

Are you a monster?

No, I'm a ❷ _____ .

Are you a monster?

No, I'm a ❸ _____   ❹ _____ .

Are you a ❺ _____  ?

Yes, I'm a ❻ _____ monster.

Game and Activity

그림에 맞는 낱말을 골라 동그라미하세요.

①
lamp
lamb

②
big
bag

③
real
relax

④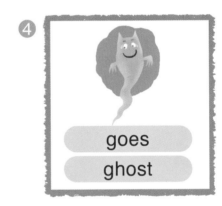
goes
ghost

⑤
snake
sneak

⑥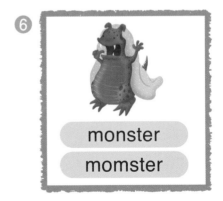
monster
momster

Before Reading

New Words 새 단어

today

tomorrow

Christmas

doll

hairpin

scarf

Key Expression 주요 표현

Tomorrow is Christmas.

❶ _____ is today.

❷ _____ is next week.

❸ _____ is next month.

Christmas gift

What's the date today?

It's December 24th.

Tomorrow is Christmas.

Merry Christmas, Sally.

What do you want?

I want a doll.

I want a hairpin.

I want a scarf.

Match the Words 낱말 연결하기

①  •   • today

②  •   • tomorrow

③  •   • Christmas

④  •   • doll

⑤  •   • scarf

⑥  •   • hairpin

After Reading

Look and Choose 그림 보고 고르기

1

A: What's the _____ today?

B: It's September, 13th.

    a. day   b. date   c. tomorrow

2

_____ Christmas.

a. Hello   b. How   c. Merry

3

I want a _____.

a. doll   b. hairpin   c. scarf

Think and Choose 문장 읽고 고르기

1 This story is about _____.

    a. day   b. birthday   c. Christmas

2 When is Christmas?

    a. December 24th b. December 25th c. December 30th

Look and Write 그림 보고 쓰기

| doll tomorrow scarf today hairpin Christmas |

What's the date ❶_____ ?

It's December 24th.

❷_____ is ❸_____ .

Merry Christmas, Sally.

What do you want?

I want a ❹_____ .

I want a ❺_____ .

I want a ❻_____ .

Game and Activity

 그림으로 제시된 단어들을 찾아서 표시하세요.

① 　② 　③

a	w	i	d	s	z	o	t	m
f	x	t	o	d	a	y	o	j
v	z	q	l	h	d	j	m	q
c	y	r	l	z	k	u	o	r
h	a	i	r	p	i	n	r	u
x	q	w	t	b	n	y	r	h
z	s	c	a	r	f	h	o	n
t	v	c	h	s	j	x	w	b
c	h	r	i	s	t	m	a	s

④ 　⑤ 　⑥

New Words 새 단어

knock

who

grandma

grandpa

uncle

aunt

Key Expression 주요 표현

A: Who is there?
B: It's aunt.

A: _____ is there?

B: It's grandma.

Knock, knock

Knock, knock. Who is there?

It's grandma, Sam.

Knock, knock. Who is there?

It's grandpa, Sam.

Knock, knock. Who is there?

It's uncle, Sam.

Knock, knock. Who is there?

It's aunt, Sam.

Vocabulary

Match the Words 낱말 연결하기

 ① •   • grandma

 ② •   • grandpa

 ③ •   • knock

 ④ •   • uncle

 ⑤ •   • aunt

 ⑥ •   • who

After Reading

Look and Choose 그림 보고 고르기

①

A: Who is there?

B: It is _____.

    a. I   b. It's   c. grandma

②

A: Who is _____?

B: It's aunt, Sam.

    a. this   b. here   c. there

Think and Choose 문장 읽고 고르기

① This story is about _____.

    a. belling   b. kicking   c. knocking

② Who is not there?

    a. mom   b. aunt   c. uncle

Look and Write 그림 보고 쓰기

| grandpa   uncle   grandma   aunt   who   knock |

Knock, knock. ❶ _____ is there?

It's ❷ _____ , Sam.

Knock, knock. Who is there?

It's ❸ _____ , Sam.

Knock, knock. Who is there?

It's ❹ _____ , Sam.

❺ _____ , knock. Who is there?

It's ❻ _____ , Sam.

Game and Activity

 순서가 뒤섞인 알파벳을 알맞게 배열하여 쓰세요.

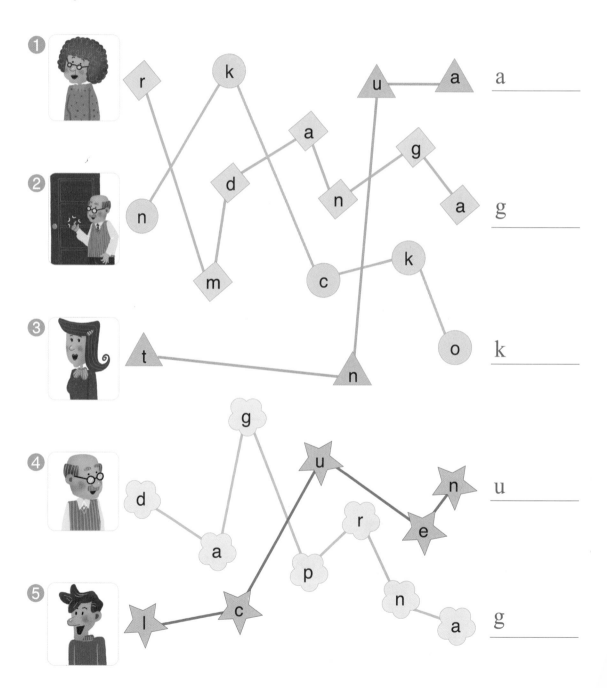

a _____

g _____

k _____

u _____

g _____

Before Reading

New Words 새 단어

rabbit

gray

pink

name

carrot

cabbage

Key Expression 주요 표현

I have two rabbits.

❶ I have three _____.

❷ I have four _____.

❸ I have five _____.

Rabbits

I have two rabbits.

One rabbit is gray.

The other rabbit is pink.

Let's give them names.

The gray rabbit's name is "Henny".

The pink rabbit's name is "Penny".

Henny likes carrots.

Penny likes cabbages.

Match the Words 낱말 연결하기

①  •　　　　　•　rabbit

②  •　　　　　•　gray

③  •　　　　　•　pink

④  •　　　　　•　carrot

⑤  •　　　　　•　cabbage

⑥  •　　　　　•　name

After Reading

Look and Choose 그림 보고 고르기

1 I have _____ rabbits.

    a. two   b. three   c. four

2 The _____ rabbit's name is "Penny."

    a. gray   b. pink   c. red

3 Henny _____ carrots.

    a. like   b. likes   c. has

Think and Choose 문장 읽고 고르기

1 This story is about _____.

    a. names   b. rabbits   c. carrots

2 What is the name of the gray rabbit?

    a. Henny   b. Penny

Look and Write 그림 보고 쓰기

pink cabbages rabbits gray carrots names

I have two ❶ _____ .

One rabbit is ❷ _____ .

The other rabbit is ❸ _____ .

Let's give them ❹ _____ .

The gray rabbit's name is "Henny."

The pink rabbit's name is "Penny."

Henny likes ❺ _____ .

Penny likes ❻ _____ .

Game and Activity

 그림을 보고 퍼즐의 빈칸을 채우세요.

①
②
③

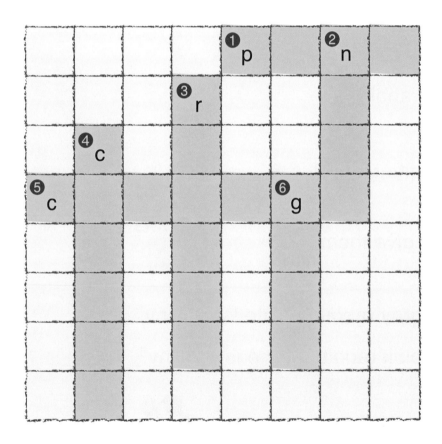

④
⑤
⑥

Before Reading

New Words 새 단어

green

T-shirt

brown

vest

blue

shoes

yellow

socks

Key Expression 주요 표현

A: What do you see?
B: I see blue shoes.

A: _____ do you see?

B: I see a brown vest.

Look at me!

Look at me! What do you see?

I see a green T-shirt.

Look at me! What do you see?

I see a brown vest.

Look at me! What do you see?

I see blue shoes.

Look at me! What do you see?

I see yellow socks.

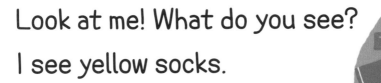

Vocabulary

Match the Words 낱말 연결하기

①    •   • green

②   •   • vest

③   •   • yellow

④   •   • shoes

⑤    •   • socks

⑥   •   • T-shirt

After Reading

Look and Choose 그림 보고 고르기

1

A: What do you see?

B: I see a green _____.

a. vest　　b. socks　　c. T-shirt

2

_____ at me.

a. See　　b. Look　　c. Watch

3

I see _____ socks.

a. blue　　b. green　　c. yellow

Think and Choose 문장 읽고 고르기

1 This story is about _____ and clothes.

a. hat　　b. color　　c. friends

2 What color is the vest?

a. yellow　　b. green　　c. brown

Look and Write 그림 보고 쓰기

shoes   green   socks   vest   T-shirt   blue

Look at me! What do you see?

I see a ❶ _____ ❷ _____ .

Look at me! What do you see?

I see a brown ❸ _____ .

Look at me! What do you see?

I see ❹ _____ ❺ _____ .

Look at me! What do you see?

I see yellow ❻ _____ .

Game and Activity

✏️ 사다리를 타고 내려가서 그림에 맞는 단어를 쓰세요.

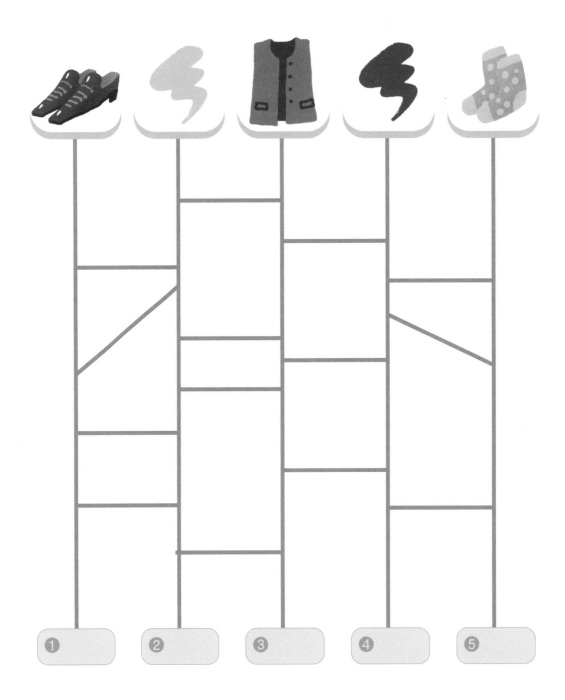

① ② ③ ④ ⑤

Before Reading

New Words 새 단어

spring

summer

fall

winter

ski

swim

Key Expression 주요 표현

A: Which season do you like the best?
B: I like winter the best.

A: Which ———— do you like the best?
B: I like summer the best.

4 seasons

There are 4 seasons in the year.

Spring, summer, fall and winter.

Which season do you like the best?

I like winter the best.

I like skiing.

How about you?

I like summer the best.

I like swimming.

Vocabulary

Match the Words 낱말 연결하기

 ①　　　　　　•　　　　　　• spring

 ②　　　　　　•　　　　　　• summer

 ③　　　　　　•　　　　　　• fall

 ④　　　　　　•　　　　　　• winter

 ⑤　　　　　　•　　　　　　• swim

 ⑥　　　　　　•　　　　　　• ski

After Reading

Look and Choose 그림 보고 고르기

1 There are 4 seasons in the _____.

    a. day   b. month   c. year

2 A: Which season do you like the best?

    B: I _____ winter the best.

    a. am   b. have   c. like

3 Spring, _____, fall and winter.

    a. sammer   b. summer   c. sommer

Think and Choose 문장 읽고 고르기

1 This story is about _____.

    a. winter   b. year   c. season

2 Which season does the boy like the best?

    a. spring   b. fall   c. winter

Look and Write 그림 보고 쓰기

spring   swimming   winter   skiing   summer

There are 4 seasons in the year.

❶ _____ , summer, fall and winter.

Which season do you like the best?

I like ❷ _____ the best.

I like ❸ _____ .

How about you?

I like ❺ _____ the best.

I like ❻ _____ .

Game and Activity

 그림을 보고 알맞은 낱말을 골라 동그라미하세요.

①

| same | swim |

②

| winter | wintar |

③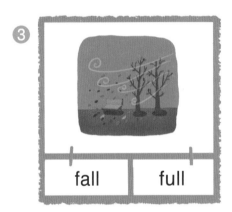

| fall | full |

④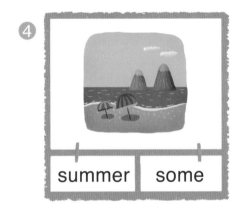

| summer | some |

⑤

| spring | spking |

⑥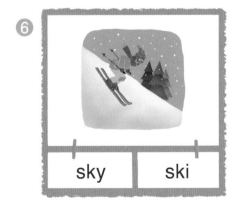

| sky | ski |

Before Reading

New Words 새 단어

vegetable

potato

onion

eggplant

cucumber

cut

make

salad

eat

Key Expression 주요 표현

Cut these vegetables.

❶ _____ these onions.

❷ _____ these potatoes.

❸ _____ these eggplants.

 **Story**

A salad

There are vegetables.

It is a potato.

It is an onion.

It is an eggplant.

It is a cucumber.

Cut these vegetables.

Let's make a salad.

Let's eat together.

Vocabulary

Match the Words 낱말 연결하기

①   •   • potato

②   •   • onion

③   •   • eggplant

④   •   • cucumber

⑤   •   • vegetable

⑥   •   • salad

Look and Choose 그림 보고 고르기

1 It is an _____.

a. onion   b. potato   c. cucumber

2  _____ these vegetables.

a. Cut   b. To cut   c. Cutting

Think and Choose 문장 읽고 고르기

1 This story is about _____.

a. Buying vegetables

b. Cutting vegetables

c. Making a salad

2 How many kind of vegetables are there?

a. two   b. three   c. four

Look and Write 그림 보고 쓰기

| cut | potato | make | onion | eggplant | eat |

There are vegetables.

It is a ❻ _____ .

It is an ❻ _____ .

It is an ❺ _____ .

It is a cucumber.

❹ _____  these vegetables.

Let's ❸ _____  a salad.

Let's ❶ _____ together.

Game and Activity

 그림으로 제시된 단어들을 찾아서 표시하세요.

①   **②**   **③**

v	s	c	p	v	p	r
c	a	e	a	t	o	u
u	w	m	o	y	t	m
t	g	s	a	l	a	d
h	m	a	k	e	t	c
i	p	o	n	i	o	n

④    **⑤**    **⑥**

Before Reading

New Words 새 단어

snow

mittens

cold

coat

rain

umbrella

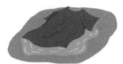

wet

sneakers

Key Expression 주요 표현

Put on your mittens.

❶ _____ _____ your coat.

❷ _____ _____ your sneakers.

Put on your mittens.

Mom, it is snowing.

Put on your mittens.

Mom, I'm cold.

Put on your coat.

It is raining.

Take your umbrella.

Mom, I'm wet.

Take off your sneakers.

Match the Words 낱말 연결하기

①  • • snow

②  • • rain

③  • • mittens

④  • • coat

⑤ • • umbrella

⑥  • • sneakers

Look and Choose 그림 보고 고르기

1 It is _____

a. snow   b. snows   c. snowing

2 Put _____ your mittens.

a. on   b. off   c. over

3 Mom, I'm _____.

a. wet   b. cold   c. rain

Think and Choose 문장 읽고 고르기

1 This story is about _____.

a. putting on   b. snowing   c. raining

2 It rains. What do you need?

a. coat   b. mittens   c. umbrella

Look and Write 그림 보고 쓰기

wet umbrella mittens sneakers cold coat

Mom, it is snowing.

    Put on your ❶ _____ .

Mom, I'm ❷ _____ .

    Put on your ❸ _____ .

It is raining.

    Take your ❹ _____ .

Mom, I'm ❺ _____ .

    Take off your ❻ _____ .

✏️ 순서가 뒤섞인 알파벳을 알맞게 배열하여 쓰세요.

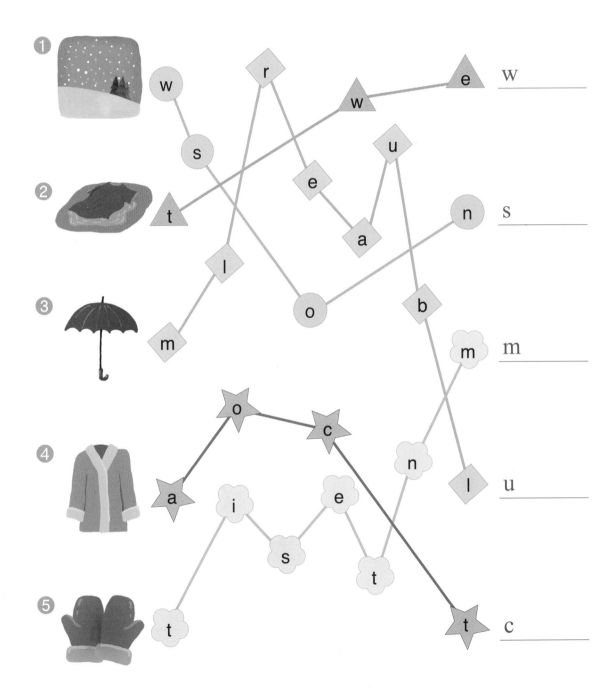

1. w _____

2. s _____

3. m _____

u _____

c _____

Before Reading

New Words 새 단어

sea

dolphin

octopus

turtle

shark

fish

Key Expression 주요 표현

This is a shark.

❶ _____ is a turtle.

❷ _____ is a whale.

❸ _____ is an octopus.

In the sea

Look at the sea!

What are in the sea?

This is a dolphin.

This is an octopus.

That is a turtle.

That is a shark.

They swim very well.

There are lots of fish in the sea.

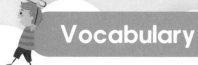

Vocabulary

Match the Words 낱말 연결하기

1    •   • dolphin

2    •   • octopus

3    •   • turtle

4    •   • shark

5    •   • sea

6    •   • fish

After Reading

Look and Choose 그림 보고 고르기

❶

_____ at the sea!

a. See   b. Look   c. Watch

❷

A: What is that?

B: That is a _____.

a. shark   b. turtle   c. dolphin

Think and Choose 문장 읽고 고르기

❶ This story is about _____.

a. the sea   b. the water   c. the sky

❷ What are in the sea?

a. fish   b. birds   c. animals

Look and Write 그림 보고 쓰기

shark   octopus   sea   turtle   dolphin   fish

Look at the ❶ _____ !

What are in the sea?

This is a ❷ _____ .

This is an ❸ _____ .

That is a ❹ _____ .

That is a ❺ _____ .

They swim very well.

There are lots of ❻ _____ in the sea.

Game and Activity

✏️ 그림을 보고 퍼즐의 빈칸을 채우세요.

①    ②    ③

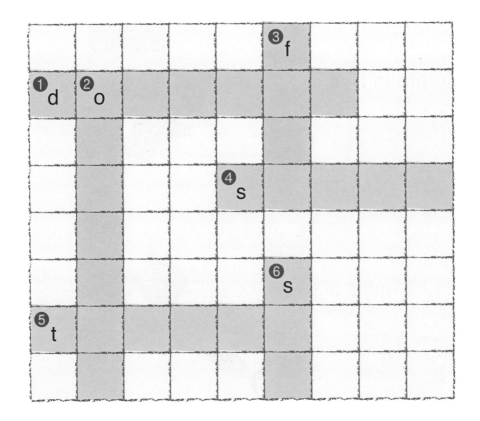

④    ⑤    ⑥

Before Reading

New Words 새 단어

pets

kitten

puppy

sofa

pretty

table

Key Expression 주요 표현

A: Where is the kitten?
B: It is on the sofa.

A: _____ is the puppy?

B: It is on the table.

I have many pets.

Do you have pets?

Yes, I have a kitten and a puppy.

Where is the kitten?

It is on the sofa.

What a pretty kitten!

Where is the puppy?

It is under the table.

What a cute puppy!

Vocabulary

Match the Words 낱말 연결하기

 •   • pets

 •   • puppy

 •   • kitten

 •   • pretty

 •   • table

 •   • sofa

After Reading

Look and Choose 그림 보고 고르기

1

A: Do you have _____?

B: Yes, we have pets.

    a. toy   b. pets   c. sneakers

2

A: Where is the _____?

B: It is on the sofa.

    a. puppy   b. kitten   c. rabbit

Think and Choose 문장 읽고 고르기

1 This story is about _____.

    a. pets   b. puppy   c. animals

2 Where is the kitten?

    a. on the desk   b. on the sofa   c. under the table

Look and Write 그림 보고 쓰기

> pretty   pets   sofa   kitten   puppy   table

Do you have ❶ _____ ?

Yes, I have a kitten and a puppy.

Where is the ❷ _____ ?

It is on the ❸ _____ .

What a ❹ _____ kitten!

Where is the ❺ _____ ?

It is under the ❻ _____ .

What a cute puppy!

Game and Activity

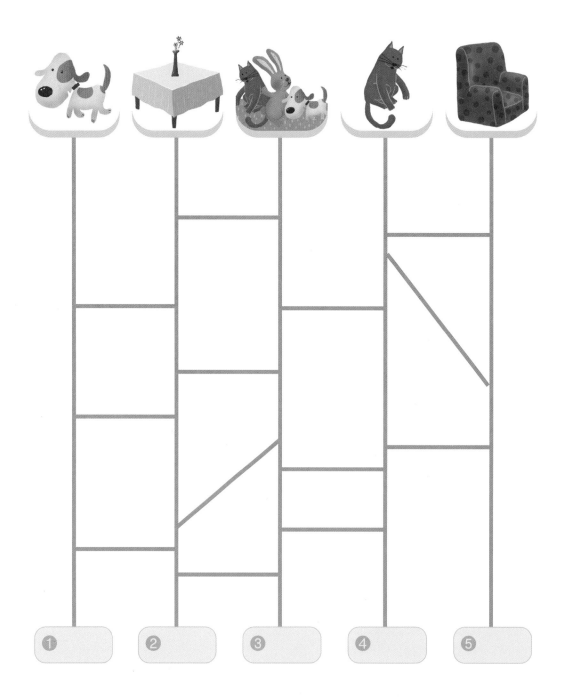

사다리를 타고 내려가서 그림에 맞는 단어를 쓰세요.

① ② ③ ④ ⑤

Before Reading

New Words 새 단어

pear

these

plum

pineapple

those

grapes

Key Expression 주요 표현

I want a pear.

❶ I _____ a plum.

❷ I _____ grapes.

❸ I _____ a pineapple.

Yummy!

This is a pear.

These are plums.

That is a pineapple.

Those are grapes.

Mom, I want a pear.

Let's wash it.

It looks yummy.

Try some.

Match the Words 낱말 연결하기

1  •   • plum

2  •   • pineapple

3  •   • these

     • grapes

4 •

5 •   • pear

6  •   • those

After Reading

Look and Choose 그림 보고 고르기

1

That is a _____ .

a. apple   b. orange   c. pineapple

2

I _____ a pear.

a. sing   b. want   c. knock

3

It looks _____ .

a. pretty   b. yummy   c. sleepy

Think and Choose 문장 읽고 고르기

1 This story is about _____ .

a. eating fruit   b. buying fruit   c. washing fruit

2 What does the boy want?

a. plum   b. pear   c. pineapple

Look and Write 그림 보고 쓰기

```
these   pear   plums   those   grapes   pineapple
```

This is a ❶ _____ .

❷ _____ ❸ _____ are.

That is a ❹ _____ .

❺ _____ are ❻ _____ .

Mom, I want a pear.

Let's wash it.

It looks yummy.

Try some.

Game and Activity

 그림을 보고 알맞은 낱말을 골라 동그라미하세요.

①
these
this

②
peach
grapes

③
bear
pear

④
pineapple
banana

⑤
plum
plue

⑥
those
fruit

Before Reading

New Words 새 단어

book

mine

this

necklace

that

mom

Key Expression 주요 표현

A: Is this yours?
B: Yes, it's mine.

A: Is this yours?

B: No, it's not _____.

It is mine.

Whose book is this?

Is this yours?

Yes, it's mine.

Whose necklace is that?

Is that yours?

No, it's not mine.

It is mom's necklace.

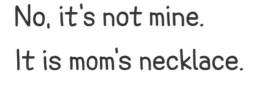

Vocabulary

Match the Words 낱말 연결하기

①    • book

②    • mine

③    • necklace

④    • mom

⑤    • this

⑥    • that

After Reading

Look and Choose 그림 보고 고르기

❶

A: Is this _____?

B: Yes, it's mine.

a. you   b. your   c. yours

❷

A: Whose necklace is that?

B: It's _____ necklace.

a. mom's   b. baby's   c. friend

Think and Choose 문장 읽고 고르기

❶ A: Is this yours?

B: Yes, it's _____.

a. mine   b. yours   c. hers

❷ A: Is that yours?

B: No, it's not mine.

It is _____ necklace.

a. mine   b. mom's   c. sister

Look and Write 그림 보고 쓰기

| necklace | book | this | mom's | that | mine |

Whose ❶ _____ is this?

Is ❷ _____ yours?

Yes, it's ❸ _____ .

Whose ❹ _____ is that?

Is ❺ _____ yours?

No, it's not mine.

It is ❻ _____ necklace.

Game and Activity

그림으로 제시된 단어들을 찾아서 표시하세요.

①   ②  ③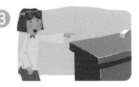

y	w	o	t	h	i	s	r
q	x	m	z	c	v	y	m
b	o	o	k	u	t	f	i
g	j	m	b	a	h	s	n
n	e	c	k	l	a	c	e
f	m	t	c	h	t	r	l

④  ⑤  ⑥

Before Reading

New Words 새 단어

birthday

candle

9

nine

blow

give

gift

Key Expression 주요 표현

A: How many candles?
B: nine.

A: How _____ gifts?

B: Three.

The birthday party

Today is Peter's birthday.

We have a birthday party for Peter.

Let's light the candles.

How many candles?

One, two, three, ... nine.

Peter, blow out the candles.

Clap, clap, clap ....

We give birthday gifts to Peter.

Vocabulary

Match the Words 낱말 연결하기

① 9 •   • nine

② •   • give

③  •   • candle

④  •   • gift

⑤ •   • blow

⑥  •   • birthday

After Reading

Look and Choose 그림 보고 고르기

①

Let's _____ the candles.

a. fire　　　b. make　　　c. light

②

Let's _____ out the candles.

a. wind　　　b. blow　　　c. go

③

We _____ birthday gifts to Peter.

a. give　　　b. cut　　　c. swim

Think and Choose 문장 읽고 고르기

① This story is about _____.

a. cake　　　b. candles　　　c. birthday party

② How many candles?

a. six　　　b. seven　　　c. nine

Look and Write 그림 보고 쓰기

| candles   nine   birthday   give   blow |

Today is Peter's birthday.

We have a ❶ _____  party for Peter.

Let's light the ❷ _____ .

How many candles?

One, two, three, ... ❸ _____ **9** .

Peter, ❹ _____ out the candles.

Clap, clap, clap ......

We ❺ _____ birthday gifts to Peter.

Game and Activity

 순서가 뒤섞인 알파벳을 알맞게 배열하여 쓰세요.

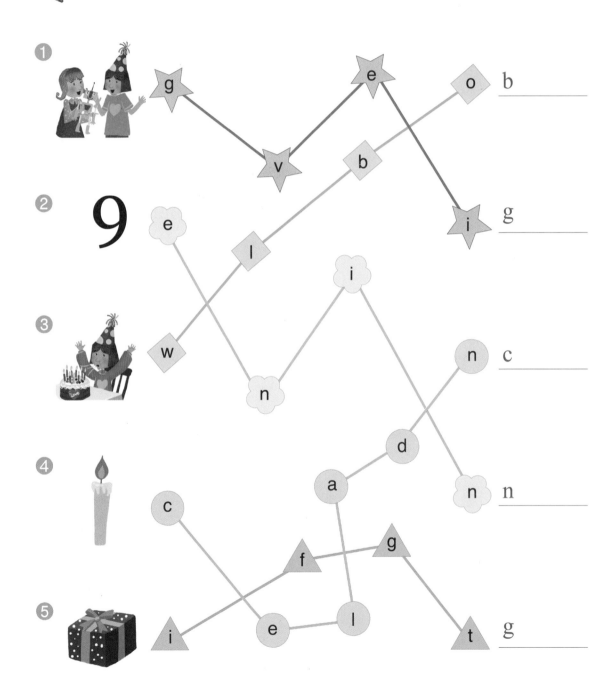

① b _____

② g _____

③ c _____

④ n _____

⑤ g _____

Before Reading

New Words 새 단어

candy

taste

sweet

chocolate

bitter

lemon

sour

Key Expression 주요 표현

A: How does it taste?
B: It is sweet.

A: How does it _____?

B: It is sour.

It is sweet.

This is a candy.

How does it taste?

It is sweet.

This is a chocolate.

How does it taste?

It is sweet and bitter.

Oh, don't eat! It's a lemon.

Oops, it's too sour.

Vocabulary

Match the Words 낱말 연결하기

1  •   • taste

2 •   • bitter

3  •   • chocolate

4  •   • candy

5 •   • sour

6  •   • sweet

After Reading

Look and Choose 그림 보고 고르기

1

This is a _____.

a. candy   b. lemon   c. chocolate

2

A: How does it taste?

B: It is _____.

a. sour   b. sweet   c. bitter

3

It's a _____.

a. pear   b. apple   c. lemon

Think and Choose 문장 읽고 고르기

1 This story is about _____.

a. color   b. candy   c. taste

2 How does the chocolate taste?

a. sour   b. sweet and sour   c. sweet and bitter

Look and Write 그림 보고 쓰기

| lemon candy bitter sour chocolate sweet |

This is a ❶ _____ .

How does it taste?

It is ❷ _____ .

This is a ❸ _____ .

How does it taste?

It is sweet and ❹ _____ .

Oh, don't eat! It's a ❺ _____ .

Oops, it's too ❻ _____ .

Game and Activity

 그림을 보고 퍼즐의 빈칸을 채우세요.

① 　② 　③

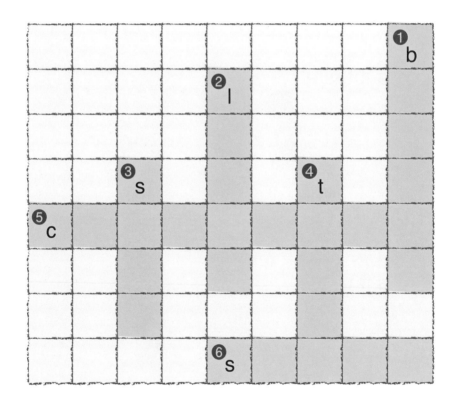

④ 　⑤ 　⑥

Before Reading

New Words 새 단어

ant

sunflower

ladybug

cosmos

beetle

violet

Key Expression 주요 표현

There is an ant
on the sunflower.

① _____ _____ a ladybug
on the cosmos.

② _____ _____ a beetle
on the violet.

They are so cute!

Look at the sunflower!

There is an ant on it.

Look at the cosmos!

There is a ladybug on it.

Look at the violets!

There are beetles on them.

They are so cute!

Match the Words 낱말 연결하기

1  •

2  •

3  •

4  •

5  •

6  •

• sunflower

• ant

• violet

• cosmos

• ladybug

• beetle

After Reading

Look and Choose 그림 보고 고르기

❶

There is an ant on the _____.

a. violet   b. cosmos   c. sunflower

❷

A: What's _____?

B: It's a ladybug.

   a. these   b. those   c. that

❸

_____ are beetles.

a. This   b. They   c. It

Think and Choose 문장 읽고 고르기

❶ This story is about _____.

  a. insects   b. flowers   c. bees

❷ Where is the ant?

  a. on the rose   b. on the violet   c. on the sunflower

Look and Write 그림 보고 쓰기

cosmos ant violets beetles sunflower ladybug

Look at the ❶ _____ !

There is an ❷ _____ on it.

Look at the ❸ _____ !

There is a ❹ _____ on it.

Look at the ❺ _____ !

There are ❻ _____ on them.

They are so cute!

✏️ 사다리를 타고 내려가서 그림에 맞는 단어를 쓰세요.

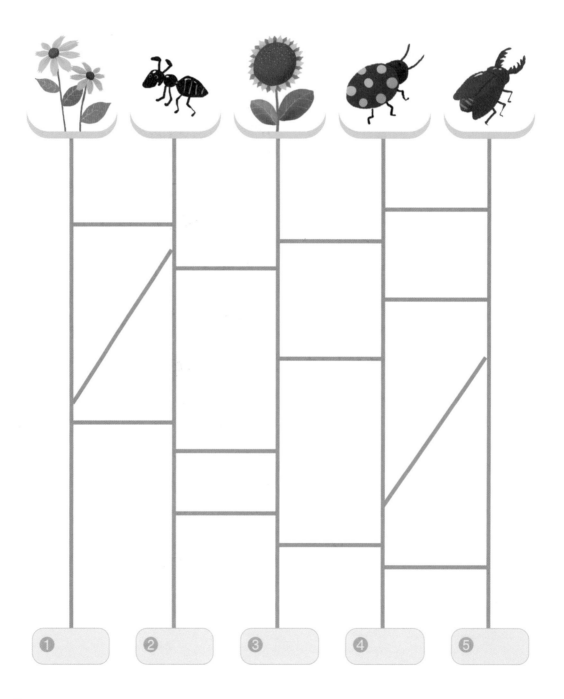

1   2   3   4   5

Before Reading

New Words 새 단어

clock

circle

TV

square

star

triangle

Key Expression 주요 표현

A: What shape is this?
B: It is a star.

A: What _____ is this?

B: It is a square.

What shape is this?

There are many shapes in my house.

What shape is the clock?

It is a circle.

What shape is the TV?

It is a square.

What shape is the frame?

It is a star.

What shape is the vase?

It is a triangle.

Vocabulary

Match the Words 낱말 연결하기

1 •   • square

2 •   • star

3 •   • triangle

4  •   • circle

5  •   • TV

6 •   • clock

After Reading

Look and Choose 그림 보고 고르기

❶

A: What shape is that?

B: It is a _____.

    a. star   b. circle   c. square

❷

A: What shape is the _____?

B: It is a circle.

    a. TV   b. vase   c. clock

Think and Choose 문장 읽고 고르기

❶ This story is about _____.

    a. star   b. circle   c. shape

❷ What shape is the vase?

    a. triangle   b. square   c. circle

Look and Write 그림 보고 쓰기

There are many shapes in my house.

What shape is the ❶ _____ ?

It is a ❷ _____ .

What shape is the ❸ _____ ?

It is a ❹ _____ .

What shape is the frame?

It is a ❺ _____ .

What shape is the vase?

It is a ❻ _____ .

✏️ 그림을 보고 알맞은 낱말을 골라 동그라미하세요.

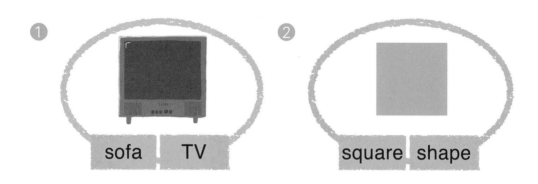

① sofa TV

② square shape

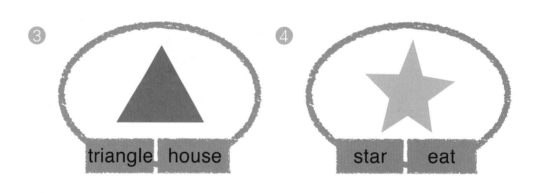

③ triangle house

④ star eat

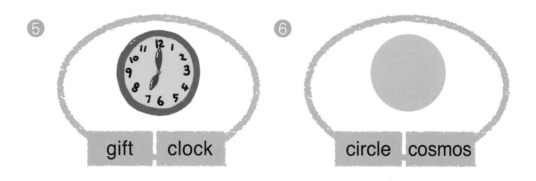

⑤ gift clock

⑥ circle cosmos

스토리 해석 및 정답

Unit 1

Key Expression   9p

time

Story   10p

몇 시예요?

몇 시예요, 엄마?
7시야.
학교에 갈 시간이란다!
오, 서둘러야겠어요.
몇 시예요, 아빠?
10시구나.
잠 잘 시간이야!
너무 졸려요.

Vocabulary   11p

Match the Words

1 seven   2 time   3 ten
4 dad   5 sleepy   6 hurry

After Reading   12~13p

Look and Choose

1 a   2 b   3 c

Think and Choose

1 b   2 b

Look and Write

1 time   2 seven   3 hurry
4 dad   5 ten   6 sleepy

Game and Activity   14p

s	l	x	z	t	a	c
t	e	n	d	i	w	s
q	t	v	k	m	j	h
y	b	h	e	e	i	u
f	z	t	b	n	r	r
r	d	a	d	v	l	r
a	s	l	e	e	p	y

Unit 2

Key Expression   15p

1 2 3 live

Story   16p

동물들은 어디에 사니?

박쥐들은 어디서 사니?
동굴에서 살아.
벌들은 어디에 사니?
벌집에서 살아.
새들은 어디에 사니?

둥지에서 살아.
개구리들은 어디에 사니?
연못에서 살아.

 Vocabulary   17p

Match the Words

1. pond   2. hive
3. nest   4. frog
5. cave   6. bee

 After Reading   18~19p

Look and Choose

1. b   2. c

Think and Choose

1. c   2. b

Look and Write

1. caves   2. bees
3. hives   4. nests
5. frogs   6. ponds

 Game and Activity   20p

1. nest   2. frog
3. bat   4. pond
5. cave

Unit 3

Key Expression   21p

Are

 Story   22p

너 피곤하니?
너 피곤하니?
아니, 그렇지 않아.
너 배고프니?
아니, 나 배불러.
너 목마르니?
아니, 나 아파.
너 화났니?
응, 그래.

Vocabulary   23p

Match the Words

1. thirsty   2. angry   3. full
4. sick   5. hungry   6. tired

After Reading   24~25p

Write T or F.

1. F   2. F   3. T

Look and Choose

1. c   2. a

Look and Write

1. tired   2. hungry   3. full
4. thirsty   5. sick   6. angry

Game and Activity   26p

① hungry   ② full   ③ angry
④ tired   ⑤ thirsty   ⑥ sick

Unit 4

Key Expression   27p

①②③ can

 Story   28p

나는 노래를 부를 수 있어요.

나는 노래를 부를 수 있어요.
라, 라! 라, 라!
샐리는 박수를 칠 수 있어요.
짝, 짝! 짝, 짝!
샘은 종을 울릴 수 있어요.
딩, 동! 딩, 동!
우리는 발구르기를 할 수 있어요.
쿵, 쿵! 쿵, 쿵!

 Vocabulary   29p

Match the Words

① song   ② ring   ③ clap
④ sing   ⑤ stomp   ⑥ bell

 **After Reading**   30~31p

Look and Choose

① b   ② a   ③ a

Think and Choose

① c   ② b

Look and Write

① sing   ② song   ③ clap
④ ring   ⑤ bell   ⑥ stomp

 Game and Activity   32p

① song   ② sing   ③ clap
④ ring   ⑤ bell

Unit 5

Key Expression   33p

monster

Story   34p

너는 괴물이니?

너는 괴물이니?
아니, 나는 뱀이야.
너는 괴물이니?
아니, 나는 양이야.
너는 괴물이니?
아니, 나는 커다란 유령이야.
너는 괴물이니?
그래, 내가 진짜 괴물이야.

Vocabulary　35p

Match the Words

① lamb ② monster ③ big
④ real ⑤ ghost ⑥ snake

After Reading　36~37p

Look and Choose

① c ② c ③ a

Think and Choose

① c ② a

Look and Write

① snake ② lamb ③ big
④ ghost ⑤ monster ⑥ real

Game and Activity　38p

① lamb ② big ③ real
④ ghost ⑤ snake ⑥ monster

Unit 6

Key Expression　39p

① ② ③ Christmas

Story　40p

크리스마스 선물

오늘이 며칠이니?
12월 24일이에요.
내일이 크리스마스구나.
메리 크리스마스, 샐리.
너는 뭘 원하니?
저는 인형을 원해요.
저는 머리핀을 원해요.
저는 목도리를 원해요.

Vocabulary　41p

Match the Words

① doll ② scarf
③ today ④ tomorrow
⑤ hairpin ⑥ Christmas

After Reading　42~43p

Look and Choose

① b ② c ③ b

Think and Choose

① c ② b

Look and Write

① today ② Tomorrow
③ Christmas ④ doll
⑤ hairpin ⑥ scarf

Game and Activity　44p

```
a  w  i  d  s  z  o  t  m
f  x  t  o  d  a  y  o  j
v  z  q  l  h  d  j  m  q
c  y  r  l  z  k  u  o  r
h  a  i  r  p  i  n  r  u
x  q  w  t  b  n  y  r  h
z  s  c  a  r  f  h  o  n
t  v  c  h  s  j  x  w  b
c  h  r  i  s  t  m  a  s
```

Unit 7

Key Expression   45p

Who

 Story   46p

똑,똑

똑, 똑. 거기 누구세요?
할머니야, 샘.
똑, 똑. 거기 누구세요?
할아버지야, 샘.
똑, 똑. 거기 누구세요?
삼촌이야, 샘.
똑, 똑. 거기 누구세요?
이모야, 샘.

 Vocabulary   47p

Match the Words

1 grandpa 2 grandma
3 uncle   4 knock
5 who   6 aunt

 **After Reading**   48~49p

Look and Choose

1 c   2 c

Think and Choose

1 c   2 a

Look and Write

1 Who   2 grandma
3 grandpa   4 uncle
5 Knock   6 aunt

Game and Activity   50p

1 grandma 2 knock
3 aunt   4 grandpa
5 uncle

Unit 8

Key Expression   51p

1 2 3 rabbits

Story   52p

토끼들

나는 토끼 두 마리가 있어요.
토끼 한 마리는 회색이에요.
다른 토끼는 분홍색이에요.
그들에게 이름을 지어주도록 해요.
회색 토끼의 이름은 "헤니"예요.
분홍색 토끼의 이름은 "페니"예요.
헤니는 당근을 좋아해요.
페니는 양배추를 좋아해요.

Vocabulary   53p

Match the Words

① gray   ② rabbit
③ carrot   ④ pink
⑤ name   ⑥ cabbage

After Reading   54~55p

Look and Choose

① a   ② b   ③ b

Think and Choose

① b   ② a

Look and Write

① rabbits   ② gray
③ pink   ④ names
⑤ carrots   ⑥ cabbages

Game and Activity   56p

① pink   ② name
③ rabbit   ④ carrot
⑤ cabbage   ⑥ gray

Unit 9

Key Expression   57p

What

Story   58p

날 봐!

날 봐! 뭐가 보이니?
초록색 티셔츠가 보여.
날 봐! 뭐가 보이니?
갈색 조끼가 보여.
날 봐! 뭐가 보이니?
파란색 구두가 보여.
날 봐! 뭐가 보이니?
노란색 양말이 보여.

Vocabulary   59p

Match the Words

① yellow   ② T-shirt
③ green   ④ socks
⑤ shoes   ⑥ vest

After Reading   60~61p

Look and Choose

① c   ② b   ③ c

Think and Choose

① b   ② c

Look and Write

① green   ② T-shirt   ③ vest
④ blue   ⑤ shoes   ⑥ socks

Game and Activity   62p

① shoes   ② vest   ③ yellow
④ socks   ⑤ brown

Unit 10

Key Expression   63p

season

Story   64p

사계절

1년에 사계절이 있어.
봄, 여름, 가을 그리고 겨울.
너는 어느 계절을 가장 좋아하니?
나는 겨울이 가장 좋아.
나는 스키 타는 걸 좋아하거든.
너는 어때?

나는 여름이 가장 좋아.
나는 수영하는 걸 좋아하거든.

Vocabulary   65p

Match the Words

① fall   ② summer
③ ski   ④ swim
⑤ winter   ⑥ spring

After Reading   66~67p

Look and Choose

① c   ② c   ③ b

Think and Choose

① c   ② c

Look and Write

① Spring   ② winter
③ skiing   ④ summer
⑤ swimming

Game and Activity   68p

① swim   ② winter
③ fall   ④ summer
⑤ spring   ⑥ ski

Unit 11

Key Expression   69p

1 **2** **3** Cut

Story   70p

샐러드

채소들이 있어요.
그것은 감자야.
그것은 양파야.
그것은 가지야.
그것은 오이야.
채소들을 잘라.
우리 샐러드를 만들자!
함께 먹자!

Vocabulary   71p

Match the Words

1 onion   **2** potato
3 cucumber   **4** eggplant
5 salad   **6** vegetable

After Reading   72~73p

Look and Choose

1 a   **2** a

Think and Choose

1 c   **2** c

Look and Write

1 potato   **2** onion
3 eggplant **4** Cut
5 make   **6** eat

Game and Activity   74p

v	s	c	p	v	p	r
c	a	e	a	t	o	u
u	w	m	o	y	t	m
t	g	s	a	l	a	d
h	m	a	k	e	t	c
i	p	o	n	i	o	n

Unit 12

Key Expression   75p

1 **2** Put on

Story   76p

장갑을 끼거라.

엄마, 눈이 와요.
장갑을 끼거라.
엄마, 저 추워요.
외투를 입거라.
비가 와요.

우산을 가지고 가렴.

엄마, 저 젖었어요.

운동화를 벗으렴.

 Vocabulary   77p

Match the Words

① sneakers ② umbrella
③ rain   ④ mittens
⑤ coat   ⑥ snow

                              78~79p

Look and Choose

① c   ② a   ③ a

Think and Choose

① a   ② c

Look and Write

① mittens ② cold
③ coat   ④ umbrella
⑤ wet   ⑥ sneakers

Game and Activity   80p

① snow   ② wet
③ umbrella ④ coat
⑤ mittens

Unit 13

Key Expression   81p

① ② ③ This

Story   82p

바닷속
바다를 봐!
바닷속에 뭐가 있니?
이것은 돌고래야.
이것은 문어야.
저것은 거북이야.
저것은 상어야.
그들은 수영을 매우 잘 해.
바닷속에는 많은 물고기가 있어.

 **Vocabulary**   83p

Match the Words

① sea   ② fish
③ turtle   ④ shark
⑤ octopus ⑥ dolphin

After Reading   84~85p

Look and Choose

① b   ② b

Think and Choose

① a   ② a

Look and Write

① sea   ② dolphin

③ octopus ④ turtle
⑤ shark ⑥ fish

Game and Activity   86p

① dolphin ② octopus
③ fish ④ shark
⑤ turtle ⑥ sea

Unit 14

Key Expression   87p

Where

Story   88p

나는 애완동물이 많아.

너는 애완동물이 있니?
응, 나는 아기 고양이와 강아지가
있어.
아기 고양이는 어디 있니?
소파 위에 있어.
정말 예쁜 아기 고양이구나!
강아지는 어디 있니?
식탁 아래에 있어.
정말 귀여운 강아지구나!

Vocabulary   89p

Match the Words

① pets ② kitten
③ puppy ④ sofa
⑤ pretty ⑥ table

After Reading   90~91p

Look and Choose

① b ② b

Think and Choose

① a ② b

Look and Write

① pets ② kitten ③ sofa
④ pretty ⑤ puppy ⑥ table

Game and Activity   92p

① puppy ② pets ③ kitten
④ sofa ⑤ table

Unit 15

Key Expression   93p

① ② ③ want

Story   94p

맛있겠다!
이것은 배야.
이것들은 자두야.

저것은 파인애플이야.
저것들은 포도야.
엄마, 저는 배를 원해요.
그걸 씻자!
맛있어 보여요.
먹어 보거라.

Vocabulary 95p

Match the Words

1. these
2. pear
3. those
4. plum
5. grapes
6. pineapple

After Reading 96~97p

Look and Choose

1. c
2. b
3. b

Think and Choose

1. a
2. b

Look and Write

1. pear
2. These
3. plums
4. pineapple
5. Those
6. grapes

Game and Activity 98p

1. these
2. grapes
3. pear
4. pineapple
5. plum
6. those

Unit 16

Key Expression 99p

mine

Story 100p

그건 내 거야.
이거 누구 책이니?
이거 네 거니?
예, 제 거예요.
저거 누구 목걸이니?
저거 네 거니?
아니요, 제 것이 아니에요.
그것은 엄마 거예요.

Vocabulary 101p

Match the Words

1. necklace
2. mine
3. book
4. that
5. this
6. mom

After Reading 102~103p

Look and Choose

1. c
2. a

Think and Choose

1. a
2. b

Look and Write

❶ book　❷ this
❸ mine　❹ necklace
❺ that　❻ mom's

Game and Activity　104p

y	w	o	t	h	i	s	r
q	x	m	z	c	v	y	m
b	o	o	k	u	t	f	i
g	j	m	b	a	h	s	n
n	e	c	k	l	a	c	e
f	m	t	c	h	t	r	l

Unit 17

Key Expression　105p

many

Story　106p

생일 파티

오늘은 피터의 생일이에요.
우리는 피터를 위해서 생일 파티를
열어요.
양초에 불을 붙이자!
양초가 얼마나 많이 있지?
하나, 둘, 셋 ……아홉

피터, 촛불을 꺼!
짝, 짝, 짝……
우리는 피터에게 생일 선물을 줘요.

Vocabulary　107p

Match the Words

❶ nine　❷ candle
❸ give　❹ blow
❺ gift　❻ birthday

After Reading　108~109p

Look and Choose

❶ c　❷ b　❸ a

Think and Choose

❶ c　❷ c

Look and Write

❶ birthday　❷ candles
❸ nine　❹ blow
❺ give

Game and Activity　110p

❶ give　❷ nine
❸ blow　❹ candle
❺ gift

Unit 18

Key Expression   111p

taste

Story   112p

그것은 달콤해.

이것은 사탕이야.
맛이 어때?
달콤해.
이것은 초콜릿이야.
맛이 어때?
달콤하면서도 써.
오, 먹지 마. 그것은 레몬이야.
저런, 그것은 너무 시어.

Vocabulary   113p

Match the Words
1 sour   2 candy
3 taste   4 chocolate
5 bitter   6 sweet

After Reading   114~115p

Look and Choose

1 a   2 b   3 c

Think and Choose

1 c   2 c

Look and Write

1 candy   2 sweet

3 chocolate   4 bitter
5 lemon   6 sour

Game and Activity   116p

1 bitter   2 lemon
3 sour   4 taste
5 chocolate   6 sweet

Unit 19

Key Expression   117p

1 2 There is

Story   118p

그것들은 너무 귀여워!

해바라기를 봐!
개미가 그 위에 있어.
코스모스를 봐!
무당벌레가 그 위에 있어.
제비꽃들을 봐!
딱정벌레들이 그 위에 있어.
그것들은 너무 귀여워!

Vocabulary   119p

Match the Words

1 cosmos   2 beetle
3 ant   4 ladybug

⑤ sunflower　　　　⑥ violet

After Reading　　　120~121p

Look and Choose

① c　　　② c　　　③ b

Think and Choose

① a　　　② c

Look and Write

① sunflower　　　② ant
③ cosmos　④ ladybug
⑤ violets　　⑥ beetles

Game and Activity

① beetle　② cosmos
③ sunflower　　　④ ant
⑤ ladybug

Unit 20

Key Expression　　　123p

shape

Story　　　124p

이것은 무슨 모양이니?

우리 집에는 많은 모양이 있어.
시계는 무슨 모양이니?

원 모양이야.
TV는 무슨 모양이니?
사각형이야.
사진틀은 무슨 모양이니?
별 모양이야.
꽃병은 무슨 모양이니?
삼각형이야.

Vocabulary　　　125p

Match the Words

① square　② clock　③ triangle
④ TV　　　⑤ star　　⑥ circle

After Reading　　　126~127p

Look and Choose

① a　　　② c

Look and Choose

① c　　　② a

Look and Write

① clock　② circle
③ TV　　④ square
⑤ star　⑥ triangle

Game and Activity　　　128p

① TV　　　② square
③ triangle　④ star
⑤ clock　⑥ circle